Testimonials
Keep Your Fork-Dessert
Is On The Way

Keep Your Fork-Dessert Is On The Way is a perfect book for me. What I get from Barb's book is at once thoughtful, relevant and practical. It doesn't drone on with intellectual arguments. One frequently hears that "short is the new long", and if that is true, than Keep Your Fork cuts the mustard. I can read a chapter in five minutes or twenty and there is plenty to reflect on. There is a "just do it" affirmation at the end of each chapter. Highly recommended for boomers and caregivers.

John Zeck
Tattered Cover Press- Denver, CO

Courage and Passion are what Barb Warner is all about in her delightful Keep Your Fork-Dessert is On the Way. The reader salivates over each morsel she delivers in her sage and insightful essays. Would be best to ask for a second helping!

Dr. Judith Briles author,
"YOU! Creating and Building the Author and Book Platforms - The Book Shepherd-
The Author and Publishing Expert

Barb is a very creative person who has taken her own experiences and transformed them into opportunities to help others learn and grow. You will surely find some tips on fulfilling your destiny through her wonderful new book, Keep Your Fork – Dessert is on the Way.

Joan Therese Seivert,
Founder, Connections Unlimited – Award Winning Senior Placement Services

Barb Warner skillfully uses warmth, wisdom and humor to show you how the second half of your life can be a time of unparalleled opportunities and creative abundance. Her anecdotes and stories will open your eyes to the joys and possibilities of the best years of your life!!

Rod Collins, author,
Leadership in a Wiki World

Keep Your Fork-

Dessert Is On The Way:

Savoring the Second Half of Life

Barb Warner
Cover Illustration by Janice Earhart

First published by Dog Ear Publishing
4010 W. 86th Street, Ste H
Indianapolis, IN 46268
www.dogearpublishing.net

ISBN: 978-1-4575-1769-3

This book is printed on acid-free paper.

Printed in the United States of America

Dedication

This book is dedicated to my fellow travelers in the second half of life who want to make all of their todays and tomorrows shine with the wisdom they have gathered from their yesterdays.

Thanks to Some Supportive Friends

Dr. Judith Briles, whose experience, advice and encouragement inspired me all along the way.

Marian Curtis, who reviewed much of my work and offered ideas on how to be clearer in my writing.

A'ra Blair, who combined her spiritual insights and author experience to give me inspiration.

Patti Wampach, who gave me my first opportunity to write for a wider audience.

Carol Voigts, whose constant enthusiasm and advice made me a better writer.

Mary Ann Smith, who designed a great website and held my hand while I learned about the blogosphere.

Erin Warner, my daughter, who spent many Thursday nights editing when the document was due on Friday.

Diana Guenot, who felt that I had an important message and encouraged me to continue writing.

Ann Johnson, my childhood friend, who offered her ideas from her home in New York.

Melissa Kline and the Rocky Mountain Women's Writers Group, who offered their editing skills.

Rod, Lorrie and Paul with my Sage-ing Circle Mastermind Group, who every month shared their ideas and support of my work.

Kathie Seedroff, who offered her creativity when it was time to put my writing together into a book.

And to Mr. Stanley, my high school English teacher. He would send my writing assignments back to me with all of the unnecessary words crossed out. I remember him whenever I edit my writing.

Chapter Titles

Introduction

Frightening and Enlightening

In 2007, I retired from my job in corporate America and began a frightening and enlightening new journey. The last day on the job, I was both relieved that I would soon be my own boss, yet was stumped about what I was going to do that would give my life meaning. Pieces of the first four decades of work life had been significant. However, some very profound aspects of myself had not yet been expressed. I hungered for something more.

In my earlier years, I always knew what came next. College followed high school. I then spent three wonderful years in the Peace Corps in Turkey. After coming back home, I lived in San Francisco, where my friends and I spent weekends supporting civil rights issues, anti-war sentiments and, later, the women's movement. After a move to Denver, I had various jobs ranging from being a travel agent for three months to working in customer service for a health maintenance organization for 12 years. I studied for a master's degree, feeling like that would give more meaning to my work experience. For the most part, however, working was like having to eat my vegetables. There wasn't anything that I enjoyed or embraced enough to call a career. I longed for experiences that were delicious: like climbing the Grand Canyon or buying figs from an outdoor market in Istanbul.

When age 65 was on the horizon, people began to ask me what I was going to do when I retired. I felt embarrassed, as I had never thought about it. I did feel the focus of my life changing, however. The appeal of sophisticated clothing from mall boutiques was fading. The charm of a smallish condo with very little maintenance was becoming more appealing, and the call of a corporate culture was no longer a part of my heart's calling. I understood this dynamic better when I read that it was common when we are younger to get direction for our lives from people and events outside of ourselves. As we grow older, however, our attention turns inward as we realize that is now where our wisdom truly resides.

At 65, I was healthier, more confident than ever and had learned some things about what made me happy. My heart was calling me into the unknown.

As an adult, I had read many books on the psychological and spiritual meaning of life. My home was overflowing with self-help books, but I needed a book that would help me make the most of the next chapter of my life. I wanted a book written by someone who was experiencing the second half of life, someone who wanted to embrace it as a truly stellar event. The great Sufi mystic Rumi said,

> *When setting out on a journey, never consult someone who has never left home.*

Since I couldn't find a book to fill this need, it was time I got to work and wrote one. I had never written much – let alone a book. Julia Cameron wrote, *I write to tell myself the truth.* It was time that I went searching for that truth. After a great deal of procrastination, one day I took a deep breath and started writing about how to find that place of truth. Once I began, I was amazed to find that there were many gems inside myself waiting to be mined. I found that I could write for hours and never run out of discoveries. I was hooked and have enjoyed writing ever since.

Writing has given me a voice to express out loud how I began to live the second half of life with a more powerful and positive heart. I continually learn about the possibilities of going deep – deeper than ever before – to mine the richness that I didn't know was there. Pablo Picasso said that he always did what he couldn't do in order to learn how to do it. This adventure became one of those experiences for me. Each time I go deeper, I discover a softer, more real person there. I sometimes find myself laughing, sometimes crying, but I'm always very grateful to realize the benefits that this process brings. Maybe if I could mine the gems within me, maybe I could help others do the same.

When I was young, I remember my mother saying in a dreamy way, "Ah, youth…why is it wasted on the young?" Now as I get older, I think, Ah, longeviety…why is it wasted on the old? I hear many of my peers complain about their aching joints, failing memory and just about anything else that they think is linked to getting older. If we don't want to waste the second half of life, it is important that we get to work and identify and appreciate the many new gifts that we have gathered over the years and examine carefully what we identify as limitations.

An important anchor since embarking on this writer's journey has been to make this endeavor first and foremost a spiritual experience for myself. Whenever my ego begins thinking that it has the answers, I pull myself back deep inside to where I know the real wisdom resides. Another temptation for me is believing that I have the answers for someone else. I constantly need to put the brakes on and know that the magic can only be created by each person's own soul, in the right way, at the right time. I hope if I ever come across as thinking that I am the expert on you or anyone else, that you will realize my error.

This is indeed a shifting time for all of us and may take a lot of bravery. Not all of us are blessed with optimal health, and we may wonder how long our finances are going to last. Things that were familiar to us in the past often seem strange and a bit scary. Sometimes it is easier to lay back and feel powerless. It is important to be aware, however, that we have more insight and wisdom than ever before and have the power to influence much of what we may have thought to be inevitable. If you do get depressed and feel really scared, it might be helpful to talk to yourself like you were your best friend. Invite your friend to tea, give her a hug and tell her all the strengths you see in her and the blessings that she has in her life.

We may not have a clue as to what the possibilities are, as many of our ideas stem from a culture that defines getting older as a terminal disease. This, however, is still our life and our story. It is true that we don't know how many chapters are still ours to write. But we do have new tools and added wisdom to explore these questions. We can create an exciting new venture of recreating ourselves! The yummy dessert we create will be the best for each of our appetites. It may be sweet like my mother's chocolate cake or tangy like Aunt Blanche's lemon meringue pie. It may be fresh fruit from Washington State or tiramisu from Italy. Or it may be a recipe that has yet to be created.

In the past several years, I have realized some pretty wonderful things about getting older. I am grateful to have the opportunity to share them with you. Together we can create a new generation of sages who continually amaze ourselves and all those around us.

I always enjoy hearing from fellow travelers. If you would like to get my e-newsletter, you can subscribe on my website.

www.barbwarner.com
www.barbwarner.blogspot.com
powerfultools.barb@gmail.com

What Does Age Have To Do With It?

"How old would you be if you didn't know how old you were?"

—Satchel Paige,
Pro baseball player

What Does Age Have To Do With It?

I n 1948, Satchel Paige was one of the first African-American pitchers to be allowed into baseball's major leagues. He was truly remarkable for that accomplishment, but he must have been remarkable in many more ways because he is quoted as asking this question:

> *How old would you be if you didn't know how old you were?*

This question has been with me, searching for an answer, since I first heard it.

Several years ago, as I was nearing retirement age, I recalled that in my earlier years I always knew what came next. After high school there was college, then marriage, children, and a career. There were a lot of bumps, of course, but family and society had pretty much made the big decisions for me. When I arrived at that watershed age of 65, however, people began asking me when I was going to retire. The more that I was asked about retirement, the more frightened I got. I actually had never thought seriously about it. I was healthy, more confident than ever before and had learned some things about what made me happy. However, I was frightened because I had no idea what was supposed to happen now. Did I really have to retire?

There was little written about this time in life except for the warnings:

> *To be old is to be sick.*

> *The secret of aging is to choose parents carefully.*

Those admonitions didn't seem to make much difference because:

> *Mental decline is inevitable.*

After some research, I learned some surprising facts about health in our later years. John W. Rowe, MD and Robert Kahn, PhD, authors of *Successful Aging*, reported that in a study made by the MacArthur Foundation in 1998, from 1960-1990 there had been a dramatic reduction in the prevalence of three important precursors to chronic diseases: high blood pressure, high cholesterol levels and smoking. Seventy-three percent of the population 75 to 84 years of age reported no disabilities at all. (Being several decades old, this research now would be even more positive.) If I paid attention and took care of myself, perhaps I could remain healthy for a long time.

It was interesting to note that this same study on successful aging found that only about 30 percent of physical aging could be attributed to heredity. Environment and lifestyle choices were the more significant determining factors.

Research that continues to unfold today shows that our DNA isn't static, however. Dr. Bruce Lipton, author of the landmark book, *Biology of Belief*, believes that it is our thoughts and beliefs that shape our DNA and that our DNA can change if we choose to become aware of what we believe. For instance, if I tried to be more conscious when assuming that since both of my parents had severe arthritis I would experience it too, maybe I wouldn't need to carry on that old familiar tradition. A very powerful concept!

In regard to memory loss, research continually shows that while there are several things a younger brain does better, like picking up a new language and remembering names, the older brain is quite capable of taking on new challenges, showing a great ability to change and grow. A positive outlook on life was one of the most important things I could do to keep my brain healthy and ready for learning. There were many actions I could take to maintain a sharp brain. Enjoying a sense of curiosity, participating in creative endeavors and laughing more were just a few.

With that hopeful news, I created a project: *Powerful Tools for the Second Half of Life*. I began providing workshops, talks and coaching for people who wanted to see their life and aging as a gift and an opportunity. Writing became a new passion. As I looked upon the experiences of my nearly seven decades of living, I realized that both the joyous and the painful took real courage and strength. I felt quite certain that I could go forward and create a life that gave expression to the best that was in me. In doing that, I could meet others who were on a similar journey. Together we could explore the unfulfilled potential that would bring excitement and meaning to our lives.

> *Some of us may not know that we have a conscious choice about how we age; that this can be a time to make contact with our most authentic, powerful and magnificent self.*

We have more options than ever before, a prospect that we may find overwhelming. Lacking the demands made on us by children, families and a full-time career, we now can consult that deeper part of ourselves, perhaps ignored until now, and find out what really "lights our fire" or "floats our boats." You know what I mean.

Just pretend that you don't know how old you are. Know that you now have more freedom, independence, time and knowledge – all gained from a lifetime of living – than you ever have had before. Is there a totally off-the-wall idea that comes to mind when you think of what you would like to do next? How about...

- Picking up and moving closer to your grandchildren or the ocean?
- Beginning to meditate?
- Bicycling again and training for a trip to the French wine country?
- Buying Rosetta Stone CDs to learn French?
- Coordinating a monthly gourmet cooking group?
- Working in your grandson's school?
- Buying a hammock and putting it up in your own back yard?

The excitement and challenge of the second half of life is to question everything we have ever learned about aging: what it means to our minds and bodies, what it means to our families and communities, and what it means to us emotionally and spiritually? It doesn't mean that our current thoughts are right or wrong. It means that this is the time to reconsider all of them.

If you are like me, you sometimes honestly forget how old you are and realize that it really doesn't matter anyway. With this awareness you can enjoy creating this new chapter in your life. To clarify what you would like to see in this new chapter, you might want to write about it, using colorful, passionate and detailed descriptions. Or you can color, paint or draw it.

Making a collage is helpful in visualizing and expressing what you really want to experience in your future. On a collage you can paste pictures, words or designs on a piece of paper expressing visually how you want your life to unfold. They are sometimes called vision boards. My latest collage has pictures of great authors such as Marianne Williamson, Jane Fonda and Sue Monk Kidd, interspersed with pictures of me and sayings like "Writing to Change the World" and "The Age of Miracles." My favorite is a picture of me as a baby blowing out one birthday candle and next to it is written "This Is Your Year." Be sure that if you tell friends about your vision, they are ones who believe in your dreams and will support you every step of the way.

How do you want your life to look five or ten years from now? How do you want to feel? These questions are best asked by your heart and not your head. The head is likely to be too analytical. That is certainly not needed now.

Throw caution to the wind and enjoy this opportunity to be the very creative person that you were meant to be. This truly can be a most magical exciting time of life!

Activities: There are some great journaling opportunities here. Close your eyes and breathe deeply. Create pictures in your mind. How would you like your life to look and feel 5-10 years from now? Be as specific as possible. Believe in miracles.

Affirmation: My second half of life is filled with an abundance of joy and resources . I allow good things to come to me daily.

When I'm 64

"Send me a postcard, drop me a line"

—Paul McCartney

When I'm 64

In 1967, the Beatles released the song *When I'm 64*. I remember listening to the lyrics and thinking, *Whoa! 64! That's a long time from now!* I couldn't imagine losing my hair, wasting away and knitting by the fireside. After all, only grandmothers did those things.

What people expect strongly influences how they see the world. For example, stereotypes – beliefs about specific groups of people – influence our thinking about getting older and the aging process itself. In some cultures, elders are thought to be wise, are respected and are treated as valuable assets to families and society. In our culture, elders are often described as cranky, fragile and forgetful. And many times they are not called elders but just old people.

In her books *Mindfulness* and *Counter Clockwise*, Harvard psychologist Ellen J. Langer writes about deeply embedded thoughts we have about important life events such as getting older. She calls these thought patterns *premature cognitive commitments* and notes that once these patterns are deeply fixed in our minds, we view them as truths about life. As children, if we hear that old people are cranky, fragile and forgetful, those thoughts may be stored in the subconscious and never re-examined. As a result, we may expect people, including ourselves, to waste away when their 64th birthday rolls around.

> **In the Chinese culture, elders are considered wise and valuable assets. This is in marked contrast to the American culture that tends to favor youth and devalues older adults.**

In one study, Langer studied older Mainland Chinese, hearing impaired older Americans, and mainstream older Americans to explore whether negative stereotypes about aging contributed to actual memory loss in old age. Langer's hypothesis was that older Chinese participants and hearing impaired Americans would outperform older mainstream Americans on memory tests. Her data showed a clear correlation between cultural views of aging and memory performance among these two groups. She concluded that in cultures where aging is viewed positively, elders performed better on memory tests.

In her 1979 "counterclockwise" study, Dr. Langer brought two groups of men in their 70s and 80s to a weeklong retreat that was made to look and feel like 1959. Eisenhower was president, *Gunsmoke* was on the radio and Jack Benny was making people laugh. One group was told to reminisce about the era and the other group was told to let themselves be who they were 20 years earlier.

By the end of the week, both groups showed significant improvements in hearing, memory, strength and intelligence. The group told to behave like they were 20 years younger also showed better dexterity, flexibility and looked younger, according to observers who were shown photos taken before and after the retreat.

Some short-term memory does change as we get older, but this change does not necessarily mean brain deterioration. New research shows that while younger brains can better do things like learn a new language, remember people's names or recall where car keys were placed, the older brain has a tremendous capacity to change, grow and take on new challenges.

Langer says that rather than declare failure when we are not as nimble on the tennis court or climbing stairs as we used to be, we may just have to try a few different strategies. Believing in our limitations often times makes them a reality. Internalizing negative sterotypes just may be the problem.

A lot can be done to maintain strong memory throughout the second half of life. Brain plasticity, the capacity of the brain to physically change its structure as new experiences are encountered, is an exciting development in brain health.

> *"People don't understand the extent to which brain health is under their control. They believe they are stuck with their inherited brain endowment. However, we have the ability at any point in life to do the right things to maintain brain fitness and keep our memories."*
> —Dr. Michael Merzenich, neurophysiologist at the University of California in San Francisco

Following are some simple and satisfying ways to keep your brain healthy.

- Laugh more
- Maintain a sense of curiosity
- Learn something new each day
- Find out about those who have lived long lives with vitality
- Renew your sense of purpose
- Deepen your connection to others
- Be actively grateful. Practice gratitude
- Examine your beliefs about aging, life and yourself
- Relax. Your brain works better in a relaxed state
- Sleep. Rejuvenation and stimulation enhance creative brain activity

I still love the Beatles and the song, *When I'm 64*. When I first listened to it at age 24, I couldn't imagine leaving my 20s, let alone turning 64. Now that I'm well past 64, my life seems more vibrant than ever. The thought of spending a night by the fireside knitting doesn't sound bad at all. Maybe when I'm 84.

Are there unpleasant aspects of your life that you feel are unavoidable now that you are at your current age? Is your life operating with long-standing, premature cognitive commitments that have been a part of your family story for years? Such as, everyone in our family becomes forgetful at a young age. No wonder I keep losing my car keys.

A goal for myself in the next several years is to visit France. Since a pathetic attempt in high school to learn French, I have told myself that learning a foreign language was not one of my talents. When I was in the Peace Corps in Turkey I found that speaking Turkish was most comfortable when I spoke to my language peers — my three-year-old nursery school students. My goal in learning French will be modest and limited to getting directions to Monet's Garden or the street to the nearest pastry shop. I do want to dispel the myth that I've had for years, however, that learning to speak French can never happen.

Activities: Looking back to your 20s, what did you think your life would look like at 64? Did it look bleak or joy-filled? Or did you ever look at 64?

Affirmation: I will challenge every self- limiting thought I have and ask myself how I

know that it is true. Even if it is part of my family story, even if a wise person has said it to be true, it may not be true. My thoughts become my reality.

Change:
The Magic Elixir

"When you are through changing, you are through."

—Bruce Barton

Change: The Magic Elixir

Albert Einstein was holding an exam for his university students. One of his students rushed up to him and said,

Dr. Einstein there has been a terrible mistake. This exam is the same as last year's exam. All of the questions are exactly the same.

Dr. Einstein smiled and said,

Don't worry. This year the correct answers are all different.

For those of us in the second half of life, not only are the answers different, but often we don't even understand the questions. The outside world is changing at an ever-increasing pace. Our internal world is changing quickly, too. Different things are of interest, and the opinions that were held with great

Barb Warner

intensity for years now don't have the same force and meaning as they did 20 years ago. No longer primarily identified as mother, husband, engineer or nurse, we search to find new meaning for our life.

Our children don't come to us for advice any more, and often not even our dog listens to what we have to say. At this time, there are two choices available for navigating our life. We can let events just "happen" to us. However, when there is no conscious awareness directing our lives, we may find it feeling empty and useless. Another possibility is getting up each morning and writing our own action plan for the day and creating extraordinary unique experiences. For some of us, the extraordinary may be relaxing as we sit in the park watching the squirrels play. For others it may be going on a yoga retreat to Costa Rica or writing poetry.

Surprise! There is a glorious plan in all of this. Look at yourself as an artist designing this next phase in life. Sometimes it may seem that time is running out – and in some ways, it is. However, now is actually an opportunity to go deeper into the present and stretch out time. There may be choices that are available that weren't seen earlier. Life was moving too fast to see them.

The key now is to accept 100% responsibility for our life going forward. Our future cannot be determined by the past. This is not always easy but it is essential. The only use the past has is to remind us of the important lessons that have been learned; sometimes with grace and elegance, and sometimes kicking and screaming. Those lessons are like an entry ticket to a revitalized second half of life.

> *Forgiveness of others and ourselves, as well as a sense of humor, is primary as we explore the past and bring strength to the present.*

Pain is a feeling all of us experience many times in our lives. If you are still experiencing pain from the past, this is a good time to embrace it and commit yourself to healing. Writing about it or reading self-help books may help. If it is a deeper issue, a counselor, friend or clergy person to talk with may be the perfect solution. It may seem like old stuff, but if it is still bothering you, it isn't "old stuff." And at this time in your life, you deserve to feel good! It's part of the change process.

So imagine yourself like a butterfly emerging from a cocoon. You are not the same person you were twenty years ago, only twenty years older. You are wiser and have a more profound perspective about life. Life is giving you the opportunity to experience rebirth of the soul

---

Some changes look negative on the surface but soon you will realize that space is being created in your life for something new to emerge.

Eckhart Tolle

We all resist change sometimes. Change is only painful when we resist it. Now our lives are calling on us to have more faith in our vision and in ourselves. Change calls for faith in a power that gives us real strength. Where we put our faith is where we put our power.

You may want to explore the changes in your life by asking yourself some questions:

- What are the most valuable changes you have made recently? In your work? At home? In your relationships? In your life?
- What inspired those changes?

- Can you identify the most valuable changes you would like to make in the next several months? In your work? At home? In your relationships? In other parts of your life?
- What is inspiring you to make the changes?

Congratulations on your courage to examine your life and to make meaningful changes. They may be big, like moving closer to grand-children, or small, like getting that aching tooth fixed. You may decide to get in shape and take a bike ride through France's wine country. Or maybe just learn to ride a bike. A childhood friend of mine, after being a school counselor for many years, finds her joy in singing in her church choir and watching the hummingbirds on the feeder in her back yard in rural New York.

Several years ago, an influential American educator and author, Howard Thurman, encouraged us to search for our own true selves when he said:

> *Don't ask what the world needs. Ask what you need to come alive and do that. What the world needs is people who have come alive.*

Activities: This is a great time to do some journaling in response to the questions asked earlier. When is it easy for you to make changes? What thoughts make change difficult? Is there any reason to question the validity of those thoughts? Can you forgive yourself and look at the lessons learned when your decisions don't turn out so great?

Affirmation: When it's time to make changes in my life, I go deep within for the wisdom that is waiting to be mined.

Passion As Your Guide

"Follow what you are genuinely passionate about and let that guide you to your destination."

—Diane Sawyer

Passion As Your Guide

J oan of Arc said,

> *I want to know what I was born for and I want the courage to do it.*

When it came time for me to retire from corporate life several years ago, I felt empty. I didn't know what I had been born for but knew there must be something more. I experienced some terrifying moments. I cringed, seeing myself sitting in my living room looking out the window for the next 30 years of my life. I knew there was a song inside of me waiting to be sung, but I didn't have any more information than that.

A bird doesn't sing because it has an answer. It sings because it has a song.

Maya Angelou

I realized that composing that song wasn't something that I could force to happen. I had to allow the tune, the words and the tempo to come naturally and spontaneously.

I had to trust.

In the second half of life our goals and values change. We are not the same person we were 20 years ago. Self-expression is now more important than ambition. We usually don't want to follow someone else's rules or learn things that we think are unimportant. Time is of the essence. It is about what makes us feel passionate. It's about what makes us come alive.

Passion can be perceived as frightening. It may conjure up thoughts of acting out of control, following irrational instincts and being totally and neglectfully self-involved. No wonder it engenders fear. However, in actuality, experiences that are relegated as off limits by fear are the ones that hold the most promise for discovery.

Passion can either be a pilot light that has been simmering in your soul for a while, or it can be a blinding flashing light that recently has gotten your attention. Either way, it has the potential to be life changing.

You can identify it as a passion if:

- It is an activity that, when you do it, the time goes by without you even knowing it.
- The more you focus on it, the more excited you get.
- You enjoyed doing it when you were 12 years old
- As a fiery kid you were obstinately passionate about this pursuit or pleasure, before you began to fit into the uniform of society's expectations.
- Whenever you think about it, you get a feeling (sometimes just a tickle) of familiarity and attraction.

By considering these ideas, you learn to understand yourself more fully. The process of discovering your passions is a form of purpose and passion in itself. When you begin seeing new connections, it will be so satisfying and exciting that you will be hooked and will understand the power behind all of this.

Wherever you put your passion, that is where your power is.

This inquiry drew me to writing and giving talks about our power in the second half of life. I had never had much interest in writing. However, there was some internal nudging that encouraged me. One day I sat down and began writing about not being interested in writing. One word led to another, and I began to enjoy expressing my thoughts on paper. I found that time went by, and I didn't even know it. The more focused I was on writing, the more excited I got.

Old friends and people whom I hadn't even met began to contact me after reading some of my work.

> *I can't tell you how much your article on "Change" gave me a light bulb moment. I even went on line and joined e-harmony.*
> —Pat (whom I haven't met yet)

> *I think your ideas are positive and interesting without being the least bit saccharine-a fine line indeed. So, I hope you will keep them coming.*
> —Margot (a high school friend)

Finding your passion is a very personal journey. Your passion may be similar to something you did in the workplace or it may be the complete opposite. It may take you to Africa to teach school or to your dining room table to take up scrap booking with the grandkids.

Passion can feel like a breeze or a hurricane. If you have a song that you have yet to sing, it's important to listen to messages coming your way. You may get a clue from observing or experiencing something that makes your heart jump or brings a smile to your face. Writing in your journal each day is one way to keep track of the messages and insights you receive.

Activities: What recent passions have you identified? Do they excite, scare or surprise you?

What have you done with the information you have received about yourself?

Affirmation: Going forward I dedicate myself to recalling the song I came here to sing.

Bette And Me

---

*"What is the <u>one proven</u> scientific way
to alter the effects of aging and boost
the quality of life as you get older?"*

—Dr. Gene Cohen

Bette And Me

A few months before my 70th birthday, I sat down to write this story about Bette. And me. I felt very alive and grateful for the opportunity to express my creativity by writing.

In my youth, I had made several attempts to express myself creatively. When I was 10, the church choir director, Mrs. Pearl, sent me home from choir practice. She said, "You don't sing well enough." I can grin a bit now remembering this, but at the time it was pretty awful.

Then there was Mr. Maxwell, the band teacher, who told me I could carry a horn and march in the band as long as I didn't make any noise. At age 12, after auditioning for the role of a young Native American princess, the community theater director told my mother,

"Barbara wasn't cut out for acting on the stage." And then there was Mr. Stone, my seventh grade art teacher, who said, "Your tree doesn't look like a tree." (I think many of us had the same art teacher in the 1950s.)

So here I am, 60 years later, to tell those of you who had experiences similar to mine—there is hope! Scientific research has revealed that creativity is an ever-developing and dynamic aspect of our growth.

Dr. Gene D. Cohen says in his book, *The Creative Age: Awakening Human Potential in the Second Half of Life*:

> *Different than many other cells in our body, brain cells called neurons show adaptive capacity regardless of age. It is clear that our brain function and creative potential don't diminish as other body systems do.*

This means that, like explorers, we can set out on a new journey without any limiting stories from our past. We can write new stories as we go forward.

I still love to sing. Several months ago, as I was driving home by myself from Santa Fe,

New Mexico, I spent hours singing duets with Bette Midler and enjoyed every minute of it. Sometimes I go to church on Christmas Eve and find a place between two good singers. Others sitting around don't hear me as I try blending in with the deep baritones on either side.

In my watercolor class I marvel, not at the trees in my paintings, but at the magic that appears when different colors run together in a beautiful medley. The process gives me joy.

Rather than performing on stage, I now express my creativity by facilitating interactive talks with groups on subjects that excite me. We explore what makes us come alive, the benefits of expressing joy and gratitude in the second half of life, and how we mine the wisdom we have gathered over the years.

Dr. Cohen defines creativity as an ability that everyone has to think a new thought and to act on it. He explains that when acted upon, this is, "one proven scientific way to alter the effects of aging and boost the quality of your life as you get older." So if you have ever thought that you weren't creative, think again.

Your creativity doesn't have to be in art or music. It can be fixing cars or simply the way you live your life. You can jump start your creative energy by thinking about what makes you come alive. Do you want to build on what you have done in the past and bring it forward? Do you want to move in a new direction? Do you feel that you haven't done anything particularly creative and now is the time to start? Or is there a totally outrageous idea hidden away on your secret bucket list that you haven't let surface?

In the second half of life, you have the opportunity to create new beginnings. You have a chance to question every assumption you ever made about the possibilities at this time of your life.

What makes you come alive now? Your list is probably quite different than it was 20 years ago because of the perspective and wisdom you have gained.

There may have been times in your life that you didn't live as creatively as you would have liked. You can use your newly discovered knowledge and insights to make over your life.

- If you like the idea of working with kids, there are schools, recreation centers and many other venues waiting for you to call.
- If you always wanted to be a firefighter and that wasn't encouraged, explore volunteering at a fire station.
- If both volunteering and traveling appeal to you, the Peace Corps may provide some meaningful, life-changing opportunities
- If sitting at home (or at the nearest Starbucks) writing in a journal appeals to you, run down to the nearest stationary shop and get a spiral notebook and a great pen and sit down with a latte.

Ellen Glasgow, who won the Pulitzer Prize at age 67 wrote, "In the past few years, I have made a thrilling discovery - that until one is over 60, one can never really learn the secret of living. The unique combination of creativity and life experiences creates a dynamic dimension for inner growth and the opportunity to shine in the second half of our lives."

Let's commit ourselves to heeding the advice of Hunter Thompson who famously followed his unique style of creativity wherever it led him.

Life should not be a journey to the grave with the intention of arriving safely in a pretty, well preserved body. But rather to skid in broadside, cheese danish in one hand, a banjo in the other, smiling and screaming, "Woo hoo! What a ride!"

Who is your Bette? You might ache to bake like Julia Childs. Or have a desire for outdoor activity like the Over the Hill Gang, people over 50 who enjoy hiking, biking and skiing. If singing has always been a secret desire of yours, a group like the Raging Grannies may be right up your alley.

Activities: What are your thoughts about your creativity? If you are in the second half of life, do you know that you are creative? If you have any doubts, look again at this chapter and review the descriptions of creativity. Sit with that knowledge for a while. Breathe deeply. Let your creative mind flow. Write in your journal what comes to the surface. Each day, affirm a new aspect of your creativity.

Affirmation: I allow my creativity to blossom. There are no limiting ideas from the past with any validity. Every day, I am aware of a new aspect of my creativity, and I rejoice.

A Lesson In Meaning

"Having feared death all of my life, now that I have confronted it, I no longer fear it. Had I during my life feared death as little as I do now, I would have dared more and better things."

—Rex Winsbury
(to read Mr. Winsbury's complete article,
go to www.hospice.net)

A Lesson In Meaning

Mr. Smith, there is nothing more that we can do for you. The cancer has spread throughout your body. I suggest hospice care for you, which will allow you to spend your remaining days in your own home as pain-free and comfortable as possible.

For most adults, good health and the ability to make personal choices are basic to a meaningful life. We find meaning in work, in our friends and family, and in choices that we are able to make each day. A life-limiting illness can shatter this sense of meaning and purpose. There are few challenges in life as great as helping yourself or someone else live a meaningful life while dying.

Shock and numbness are natural responses to this painful news. A person can usually only cope with this new reality in doses. It takes time to understand this news with both the head and the heart. Acknowledging the reality of this news is, however, the first step to continuing to live a meaningful life.

Hospice is a concept of care designed to provide comfort and support to patients and their families when an illness no longer responds to cure-oriented treatments. It helps patients live their last days as alert and pain-free as possible. Specially trained professionals, volunteers and family members provide this care in the home, care facility or a hospice center.

The primary goal of hospice care is to provide comfort; relieve physical, emotional and spiritual suffering; and promote the dignity of the terminally ill person. Hospice care neither prolongs nor hastens the dying process, and it focuses on the needs of both the patient and the family.

Roger Bone, MD (A *Dying Person's Guide to Dying*, www.hospicenet.org) was a physician who died at age 55 in 1997 of renal cancer. While living his last days, he wrote recommendations for others facing a terminal diagnosis. Here is my summary of his suggestions.

- *Some family members and friends will treat you differently.* Even before you show signs of a serious illness, people may have a different look in their eyes as they talk with you. They will come around to their normal selves when they get over the shock.

- *Don't be afraid to ask to be alone.* You need time by yourself.

- *However confusing that this experience is, remember that only you know what you need.* You can and should ask for information and advice, make telephone calls, read books – but ultimately it is important to make decisions that feel right to you.

- *Slow down and ask your family and friends to slow down.* There may not be a lot of time but there is sufficient time in all but the most extreme cases to think, plan, and prepare.

- *Find out as much as possible about your disease.* What is it? How will it affect you? And very important, how will it cause your death? It is helpful to have a friend participate in these discussions with your health care providers. At this time you may not be able to comprehend the answers that you are being given. (See more regarding an advocate in #7 below.) Also, the Internet, organizations such as the American Cancer Society and books may give you the information that you need.

- *Seek a second opinion.* Friends who have had a similar experience may be able to give you referrals. Sometimes your health care team can give you suggestions of other providers who they think will be helpful. When I was fifty-eight, I received a breast cancer diagnosis. I was not comfortable with my first oncologist's opinion on my course of treatment. I ended up getting three others; the last from a team of doctors at the University of Colorado Breast Cancer Center. The last three opinions were the same and following them saved me a lot of needless pain and resources.

- *Find someone to be your advocate.* My friend Carol's husband recently died. She was her husband's advocate. She cleared everything with him before decisions about his care were made and she kept people away if he was not feeling well. She said, "He wanted to use his last weeks with those he was closest to. He couldn't say that to people but I could." You may want several different advocates depending on what your needs are. Carol also says that her husband found satisfaction in writing his own obituary.

- *Regardless of your spiritual or religious beliefs, you may discover that you will be asking the question, "why"?* Your doctor or your hospice will have a spiritual person available to talk with you about the new questions that are arising.

The following are ideas shared by Rex Winsbury, a British journalist who survived a terminal cancer diagnosis. He experienced the needs and challenges of someone who was dying but lived to reflect and share them.

Consider these ideas:

- the need to "settle up" with the people that he felt close to, so as to die in peace with them and with himself.

- the importance of having someone to "stand in" for him, to do what he couldn't do if he became helpless.
- the need to know places and organizations that he could turn to for practical information.

Mr. Winsbury continued by giving us some sage advice.

- Find someone or somewhere to talk about death.
- Find someone to tell you that you are still beautiful
- Find someone who would help to restore hope, within the context of realism about the situation.
- Find someone to forewarn you and teach you about the stress of your illness upon others.

He concludes with the inspiring words on the title page of this chapter.

Activities: Often times while we are still healthy, becoming comfortable with our own death creates an atmosphere of relief and enhanced joy as we age. What are your feelings about your own death? Are

they helping or hindering your enjoyment of this time of life? Are there people you can talk to about this?

A Thought to Remember: "Some people are so afraid to die that they never begin to live." Henry Van Dyke

Perpetual Joy

"Expressing gratitude explains well-being more than any other of the most commonly studied personality traits."

—Dr. M. McCollough and Dr. Robert Emmons

Perpetual Joy

If you choose to read this be prepared to feel consistently happier than you ever have before. Be prepared to give thanks for a sunny day. Be prepared to give thanks for a rainy day, for a hot day or a cold day. Be prepared for a day with peace in your neighborhood. Be prepared to give thanks for your friends and also for those people who work to build your character by trying your patience.

Be prepared for less depression and more kindness toward people you don't even know. Also be prepared for an increased interest in things like physical fitness, healthier eating and progress toward personal goals.

Two psychologists, Dr. Michael McCollough of Southern Methodist University in Dallas, Texas, and Dr. Robert Emmons of the University of California at Davis report:

- Expressing gratitude is able to explain well-being more than any other of the most commonly studied personality traits.
- People who practice daily gratitude exercises have higher levels of alertness, enthusiasm, determination, optimism and energy.
- Life satisfaction has a much larger correlation with gratitude and much smaller correlation with age, education, income, intelligence or attractiveness.

Since beginning to study gratitude, it has become an essential part of my life. Sometimes I lie in bed at night and, starting at my toes, I give thanks for every part of my body. If I have a headache, I take an aspirin, followed by giving thanks for the many wondrous experiences that my head facilitates for me each day. When washing my hands, I give thanks for hot water and remember the times living in Turkey in the Peace Corps when there was only cold water running from the faucet. And then there are blessings to all of those in the world who don't have running water of any kind.

To increase the level of gratitude that we experience, here are a few suggestions.

1. Pay attention to good things, large and small. The other day I met a woman who had decreasing eyesight, as well as diminished hearing. When I asked her for what she was grateful for, she said, "At least I am not completely blind."

2. Pay attention to bad things that are avoided. Recently a friend fell off her bike and was so grateful that the only thing injured was her self-confidence. She knew she needed to get back on the bike as soon as possible.

3. Practice downward comparisons. When returning from a strenuous hike and feeling very achy, I can give thanks that I didn't need a cane or walker and that a hot bath and a rest will take care of the aches

4. Gratitude is a character strength that can be enhanced with practice. You can establish regular times to focus on being grateful.

5. Elicit and reinforce gratitude in the people around us. Positive moods are catching,

but negative ones can be as well. How do you tell people around you who are negative that you don't want to be around negative people without being negative yourself? Actually, now that I think about it, since I've become more positive, I haven't been around many negative people. Isn't it interesting how that works?

Probably the best known, easiest and most useful of all tools for those who want to reinforce all of the benefits of being grateful is starting a Gratitude Journal.

1. Choose a blank notebook or journal. I like a spiral-bound notebook that opens flat for ease in writing. Keep it somewhere convenient: next to your bed, in your car, at your desk. Or you might want more than one.

2. Be aware of things during the day for which you are grateful. View obstacles as opportunities to appreciate. You will attract more positive energy.

3. In the evening, review your day and include anything big or small that was a source of gratitude: flowers in bloom, good tires on your car, new hazelnut coffee, the fact that

you can see, read and write. All these allow you the opportunity to write in your gratitude journal.

4. You might have fun personalizing the gratitude journal with clips, photos, quotes, etc.

It is normal and healthy to express regret and mourn losses when painful things occur in our lives. This is essential for good mental health and must not ever be missed. When we don't acknowledge those distressing emotions, we cannot fully experience joy. I remember crying uncontrollably when my sister died twelve years ago of breast cancer. The pain went down so deep that I felt it had reached the depth of my being. It was there that I experienced release and was overwhelmed with the comfort that I felt.

When the deep pain passed, I was able to recall and be grateful for times we had spent at the beach together as kids and the nights as adults when we stayed up late talking about the meaning of God in our lives. I still talk to my sister late at night when I am having a problem that I think she could help with.

Grief and gratitude can exist together and can even enhance each other.

Most of all, it is rewarding to develop our gratitude muscles. Like with any workout, in order to receive the benefits, we need to practice regularly even when we don't feel like it. When we realize how being grateful has made our lives happier and more satisfying, we can record that in our gratitude journal as well.

It is a gift to feel grateful for being grateful.

Activities: Get a notebook. At least once a day, write things you are grateful for. In the morning it could be the opportunities that you intend to have during the day. In the evening it could be those things that happened that you feel grateful for.

Affirmation: I feel grateful for every gift in my life today.

Who Is This New You?

"Who Am I . . . Now That I'm Not Who I Was?"

—Connie Goldman, author

Who Is This New You?

Are you finding that getting older is a hard experience to figure out? Our childhood and early adult years were spent defining ourselves—trying to be good students, good parents and good community members. Having a good work ethic and being aware of how others saw us was important. In the second half of life, these activities don't have the meaning they once did. Life's priorities and values are changing, sometimes without our conscious awareness.

Perhaps the children are grown and responsibilities outside the home don't have the central role they once did. The effort to play by the rules isn't as important as living each moment of every day as authentically as possible. Rather than relying on the stock market or the direction of the housing market to determine my financial well being, it is more comforting to go within to examine personal spiritual beliefs and trust in the lessons I have learned throughout life.

As younger adults, the answers to life's important questions usually came from family, friends, our community and the media. That was appropriate then. Now it is important that we turn attention within and access our inner wisdom and power.

Where and what exactly is this *place within*? Sometimes it is called the *still small voice*. I learned to identify it as the place that comforted me when my sister and nephew passed within a month of each other. It was the softness that I witnessed recently when I saw a father cry when given a portrait of his children. It's that place that tells me that writing is my life's purpose now.

Several months ago I sent a survey to some friends who were in the second half of life. The survey asked what positive changes they had experienced in the past ten or so years.

- I am more accepting and less reactive.
- I am kinder to myself.

- I am clearer about what and who belongs in my life.
- I am more confident about putting my skills and abilities out into the world.

This probably isn't your exact list, but you may have a similar one.

How did these people become more accepting, kinder, clearer and more confident?

We are not the same person we were 20-30 years ago, only 20-30 years older. It may take some time to become aware of the many ways we are different. However, becoming aware of those things can be quite fun and worth the effort. I realize that I'm not as upset as I use to be by certain political stories. I don't get quite as worried about the price of gas or the way teenagers are acting. It is easier for me to speak my truth even though my honest opinions may seem new and out of character for some who have known me for awhile. I also appreciate little things more, like the workmen who built my favorite mountain road or the woman behind the deli counter at Safeway.

You no doubt have experienced some amazing ups and downs. There may have been times when there wasn't enough money to meet family needs or a close friend became very ill or your company needed to downsize. There was also that marvelous afternoon at the Musee d'orsay in Paris seeing a Monet painting up close or the moment you saw your grandchild take his first step. Both joys and hardships left you a stronger and wiser person.

My childhood provided the benefits of growing up in a safe, small town on the shore of beautiful Lake Michigan. Within those beautiful surroundings there was also the pain of being a chubby little girl with very little confidence.

My early adult years provided exciting travel opportunities, including three years in the Peace Corps in Turkey. I also became the mother of a beautiful daughter who still brings immense joy to my life. Included in those adult years also was the pain of a marriage filled with conflict and jobs that didn't seem to fit. However, each of these experiences gave me gifts of personal insight. Some of those gifts I am only now realizing.

When you become aware of the life-changing experiences you have had, you will know intuitively that you are wiser and your thinking has changed. You have more opportunities to fulfill dreams you never thought possible. However until those changes come to your awareness, you won't really understand their value.

As the changes come to your awareness, it is a perfect time to begin writing in a journal. Memories that you have long forgotten will surface. You may have new insights about old ideas. An answer to a long buried question may emerge. You may at last be able to make sense of situations that have been unclear for years. Will Rogers reminded us that "Even if you're on the right track, you'll get run over if you just sit there."

This is your perfect time to look at life with courage, hope and gratitude and realize that you do have unfulfilled potential. Your unfulfilled potential is truly where the excitement is. Nothing has been said or written to describe the possibilities that you now have.

If this sounds overwhelming, it is a great time to go within to that *still small voice* and ask for guidance and direction. Listen with curiosity and trust. There are some important gems waiting to be mined. Congratulate yourself on your courage and willingness to explore. The new you is waiting to be expressed.

Activities: In the past few years, have you ever said or thought something so wise that you thought someone else was talking? Have you seen strengths in yourself that you never knew you had?

Record the ways that you have become more accepting, kinder, clearer and more confident than you were 10 years ago. It's time to get to know the exceptional person you are now.

Affirmation: I acknowledge with gratitude the value of newly discovered gems within me that are waiting to be expressed.

An Interesting Life!

"There is no greater agony than bearing an untold story inside you."

—Maya Angelou

An Interesting Life!

For several years I was the director of volunteer services for a nonprofit organization serving the elderly. I asked a woman if she would like to tell some of her life stories to a volunteer who would record them for her. The woman said it would be a waste of time because she never did anything important in her life. "I just stayed at home and raised 3 foster children."

I then asked a WWII veteran the same question. He also said that he didn't have anything to tell. After some coaxing he did tell about what had happened to him in the war. He had jumped out of a fighter jet as it was being shot down by the Nazis over Belgium and spent three months searching for his company. Later he said:

I was so relieved after completing my story. Relieved! The story was inside, and I had to get it out in order to be free. I felt I was hiding my story by holding it in.

Those experiences were introductions for me into the richness of life stories. After leaving the Peace Corps in 1964, I settled in San Francisco. Living in San Francisco in the 60s, a girl from rural Michigan, was like living on the edge. I have a friend who spent those same years growing up on a farm in rural Ohio. After hearing her stories I realized how challenging those years were for her too. She was a lesbian and had to navigate between acceptance from her family and community and pursing what she needed to do for her own growth. She too was living on the edge.

If you think your life was pretty uninteresting, hear what Mark Twain had to say.

There was never an uninteresting life. Such a thing is utterly impossible. Inside the dullest exterior there is a comedy, a drama and a tragedy.

So why share our stories?

1. By learning about ourselves we become better people. We gain new respect for the skills and strengths we have developed over the years and feel more confident to explore the future.

So often in our younger years we lived each day like it was a task to be accomplished without stopping to realize the talent and courage that was needed to get through the day. Like the woman who raised three foster children, we didn't realize the strength it took when our child was ill or when we lost our job and the mortgage came due or even when we took the risk of moving to another town to work at that dream job we had always wanted.

2. We give our children and families a way to appreciate and understand in a more definitive way what makes them the unique people they are.

Several years ago I attended a concert in Denver where the group performing were Beatles impersonators. Tears welled up in my eyes as I remembered the time in the 1960s when I first heard their recorded music at a party of Peace Corps volunteers in Ankara, Turkey. Now, fifty years later, I was nostalgic, remembering the intensity and pride of being a part of that important movement. The Peace Corps had enhanced both my life and the lives of many children and families in Turkey. It felt important. I had made a difference. Perhaps the world was a bit better because of me.

After that concert in Denver, I told my young adult daughter what I had experienced while hearing the Beatles' music once again. I told her about President Kennedy's influence on my life and how spending three years as a Peace Corps volunteer was a defining time that profoundly influenced the rest of my life. Hearing the Beatles brought it all back to me. It gave me the opportunity to share with her some of my history, which is also her history and the history of our nation.

3. We are able to enliven, ennoble and enrich work places, faith-based organizations, ethnic and other groups with common interests by sharing the stories that have brought us to the place we are today.

When strangers meet because of a mutual passion, such as helping African refugees or building a church, bonds can be formed when they speak of what has brought them to this common place. There is a comfort established that enhances whatever project is involved. Former strangers often become like family. This is true of church groups, neighborhood groups, reading circles and many others.

4. By sharing our stories, we honor the wonderful people, travels, cultures and other experiences that have enriched our lives.

There is nothing more delicious than reliving the hike down the Grand Canyon with a mutual outdoor enthusiast, describing grandmother's apple pie to your son or comparing with a fellow teacher what you remember on your first day as an elementary school teacher.

Throughout history, stories have been told around campfires and wisdom circles, at the kitchen table, and in coffee houses and bars all over the world. These tales are used to pass on accumulated wisdom, beliefs and values. They explain how things were, why they were and their role and purpose. Stories are the building blocks of knowledge—the foundation of memory and learning. Rachel Naomi Remen, MD, author of *Kitchen Table Wisdom*, writes, "telling stories is not a technique, it is not an art, it is a human need."

Until recently, storytelling had lost its important position in our society. However, both oral and written stories are now experiencing a comeback. Scrapbooking has experienced a resurgence. Videos and DVDs are easy and accessible. Blogs are a popular way to communicate.

And don't ever believe that you are too young to write your life story. Tim Tebow, a famous NFL quarterback, recently published an autobiography at the age of 23. When Jon Stewart of *The Daily Show* interviewed him soon after the book came out, he asked Tebow, "Why didn't you wait to write your life story until you were 24?" It's your call. And it is all fun.

Activites: Writing your personal stories can seem foreign at first, but if the idea appeals to you, here are a couple of ideas that perhaps will make it easier to begin.

Remember a time or two when you had an experience that changed your life forever. It can be a painful one or one that brought you joy. Note the gift of the experience and how it has impacted your life. What did you learn about yourself?

Look at any decade in your life. How would you title those ten years? What were the best and worst of times?

Affirmation: Enjoying my life stories and encouraging others to enjoy theirs brings added meaning to my life.

It Feels So Good!

"Resilient people enjoy themselves like children do."

—Al Siebert, PhD

It Feels So Good!

I love the word **resilience.** It sounds like its definition: **bouncy,** `light,` flexible, *able to return to its original form after being bent, compressed or stretched.* We all can identify with feeling bent, compressed and stretched at times in our life. Resiliency can be learned. For some of us it is natural, and for some of us it has taken some tough lessons to learn how flexible we really can be. For all of us, passing of the years is a real gift. We can become more resilient as we get older.

As I was beginning to write this chapter, I received an email from Karen, a new friend that I hadn't heard from for over a month. Apparently, several weeks earlier she was in a great deal of pain and had gone to several doctors. After being put on increasingly intense pain medications, Karen still had unbearable pain. Feeling that the medical personnel did not understand the urgency of her condition, one evening she took a cab to the hospital without a doctor's authorization. She was admitted and after being discharged a week later, she wrote a letter to family and friends outlining her stay in the hospital.

In the letter she spoke about an "uncertain diagnosis, hallucinations from the medication, inexperienced hospital staff" and other unpleasant experiences.

> "Even though I was in pain and had fear of disability, even death, I was entertained observing the way the hospital worked. Even my hallucinations were interesting."

She finished the letter by observing that for three weeks, life was so interesting that she had no need to pick up a magazine or a book.

I was very moved by Karen's bravery and sincerity in describing her hospital experiences. Professionally, Karen is a career and leadership coach and planned to go to California to conduct a workshop on creativity two weeks after leaving the hospital. She became my poster friend for *resilience.*

> **Resilience is the ability to create positive outcomes in the face of adversity.**

Many experts believe that resilience is the largest predicator of longevity. Gail Sheehy, in her book *New Passages*, speaks of the strengths that we have accumulated to take us into the Age of Integrity (after 60 years). She agrees that resiliency is the most important protection one can have. People who have met and mastered most of life passages up to now are by definition resilient.

Several months ago I attended a talk by Marion P. Downs, MA, who had just written a book *Shut Up and Live...(you know how)*. Marion is a retired professor from University of Colorado Health Sciences. She wrote this book to tell younger folks what has helped her live a productive life. She is now age 92.

She, as many of us, thought her life would end as her parent's did, at 72. When she reached that age, she realized that she was there without a road map. She realized that she didn't have any guidelines to live that long. When she mentioned that to her doctor he said,

"That, my dear, is something you are going to have to work out for yourself."

That answer might have left her angry and depressed, but instead she designed a life that still "includes good sex, lots of exercise, close friends, capable doctors and intelligent eating." Now she specializes in tennis, skiing, hiking and "a passel of great-grandchildren."

Some people are naturally more resilient than others. However, research has shown that resilience is ordinary, not extraordinary. Resiliency can be learned and cultivated by everyone. Here are some traits of resilient people.

- *They stay connected and rely on others to help them survive in tough times.* Karen called in friends when she was discharged from the hospital so that they could be trained to help her at home with her recovery.
- *They're optimistic.* Experts say that negative thinking is just a bad habit, which can be worked on. It may take some work to change our habits. But it can be done.
- *They are spiritual.* When people have strong spiritual beliefs, they are less likely to become depressed. When depressed, the depression lifts sooner.

- *They are playful.* Al Siebert, PhD, author of *The Resiliency Advantage*, says, "Resilient people enjoy themselves like children do. They wonder about things, experiment and laugh." In reading Karen's letter to friends, there was lightness when she spoke about not needing magazines or books to keep her entertained as her experiences with life were taking care of that.
- *They pick their battles.* Resilient people tend to focus on things that they can influence and not spend time on things they can't control. When Karen sensed she wasn't getting better, rather than complaining about the lack of response from her doctors, she took herself to the hospital.
- *They stay healthy.* A good diet and regular exercise help repair neurons in brain areas that are particularly susceptible to stress.
- *They actively seek solutions. Resilient people quickly hone in on challenges and devise strategies for dealing with them.* When Karen realized that she was going to need help at home, she immediately gathered friends and family to help.
- *They find a silver lining.* Steven Southwick, MD, professor of psychiatry at Yale University School of Medicine, writes, "Resilient people are like trees bending in

the wind. They bounce back and use negative experiences as an opportunity to better themselves."

After several months of receiving treatment for breast cancer ten years ago, I wanted to acknowledge myself for the emotional and physical pain that I had just experienced. I took myself on a relaxing retreat to a yoga center in New Mexico. Upon returning home, I could sense and celebrate the strength and confidence that the cancer experience had given me.

Dr. Southwick calls this phenomenon *post-traumatic growth syndrome*. Often times we don't take time to acknowledge our magnificent achievements after a particularly difficult period in our life. It is important that see ourselves as the resilient person that we are.

Activities: Think about the difficult times in your life. What were the strengths that you showed? Being that you are here now reading this, you obviously showed some resilience. Don't brush it off. If you were someone else talking to yourself, I bet you would be impressed.

When you internalize the strength of your resilience, you will know that you are mightier than you ever thought and that you, too, deserve a glorious trip to New Mexico, Hawaii, or anywhere you consider heaven to be.

Affirmation: I am strong, centered and secure. When I reach to my core, there is my strength and power.

The Gift To Give Ourselves

"Forgiveness is the fragrance the violet sheds on the heel that has crushed it."

—Mark Twain

The Gift To Give Ourselves

In meeting with individuals and groups over the past several years, I am increasingly impressed with the importance that forgiveness plays in our lives. Each of our stories is deeply personal and often contain deep pain. We may harbor anger with our spouse who forgot our birthday last year, or may still feel the pain of our parents who forgot our birthday many years ago.

Because we often don't know what to do with the pain, we may bury it, lash out in rage or allow it to fester and gnaw away at our heart for years. "Forgive and forget" can easily be recited; in real life, however, it often takes a great deal of conscious effort.

> **Forgiveness is essential in living a satisfying life. Forgiveness can be a marvelous vehicle to change our life story and make our past, present and future filled with more joy.**

Forgiveness is:

Releasing the hope that the past could be anything different, so that the past does not hold you hostage.
—Oprah Winfrey

The act of pardoning somebody for a mistake or wrongdoing. It is an inner opportunity to transform painful emotions into positive, or at least, neutral ones.
—Encarta World English Dictionary.

Forgiveness is a funny thing. It warms the heart and cools the sting.
—William Arthur Ward

When I was a child, my father was the true head of our household. He was convinced that my sister and I should go to a traditional state college rather than a more liberal private school. We should major in nursing or teaching. This was to avoid the liberal thought that a more intellectual setting might expose us to. My sister became a nurse and I became a teacher.

There were other ways that my father had made his lack of confidence in my ability to make good decisions known. As a newly married adult, I was directing a preschool in Las Vegas. I was excited to do some administrative work. When my father came to visit, he told me that I might be capable enough to work with kids but I didn't have the ability to do the intellectual and important work necessary to be an administrator.

After separating from my husband, I moved back to Denver. I had a great job, making more money than ever. I called my parents, excited about the prospect of buying a house. My father said that the responsibility of owning a home was more than I was capable of and I should continue to rent.

Don Miguel Ruiz has written a very insightful book, *The Four Agreements*. In it he writes:

> *Whenever we hear an opinion and believe it, particularly about ourselves, we make an agreement and it becomes a part of our*

Barb Warner

belief system. As soon as we agree, the poison goes through us and we are trapped in a living dream of hell. We think it is all about us. Other's emotional garbage becomes our emotional garbage!

When I was finally able to analyze and understand my father's attitudes, I realized that they had little to do with me, personally. I realized that I could do a rewrite of my life and create new chapters using a different story line. I could see that my experiences in overcoming the messages from my father had made me the strong and creative woman I am today. It was time for me to write a new life story. My story—the one for my life—the one my father never saw for me.

Incidentally, in the past twenty years, I have bought and sold one house and purchased a condo. I am still owner of that condo and another home that I recently purchased jointly with my daughter. It is all good.

When writing my new life story, I realize the importance of forgiving myself and at the same time knowing that I am totally responsible for myself. Each morning I write my intentions for the day and affirm what I would like to happen. I am indeed the author of my own story. This second half of life is continuing to bring surprises.

> *The weak can never forgive. Forgiveness is the attribute of the strong.*
> Mahatma Gandhi

Benefits of Forgiveness:

- It gives us control over our lives and fosters maturity as a person.
- It gives us more physical well-being. Harboring a grudge is stressful; it causes muscle tension, cardiovascular disease, strokes and other harm to our bodies.
- It offers blessings for ourselves and others, opening our heart to grow in love and compassion.

Elements of Forgiveness:

- Acknowledge what happened. Affirm the pain and hurt. Identify the real problem. Writing down the story may be an excellent way to sort out the elements that have affected you. Be willing to embrace the pain fully, knowing you can only ease the pain by first embracing it.

- Look at the painful elements in the story that you have the power and ability to change. How can you change those?
- Look at which elements you cannot change and how you can see those differently.
- Consider the consequences of not forgiving.
- Look at what positive outcomes the event had for you. In what ways have you become a stronger person?

Forgiveness is the gift we give ourselves.
Rabbi Zalman Schacter-Shalomi

In an article in *Arthritis Today* (2004), Fred Lusken, PhD, Director of the Forgiveness Project at Stanford writes,

"You don't have to be unusually talented to forgive others or to ask for forgiveness. Forgiveness is a teachable skill. You can learn it like you learn to play the piano."

Consider the following steps:

- Commit yourself to feeling better. First and foremost, forgiveness is for your well-being.
- Seek positive goals. Instead of mentally replaying your hurt, seek a new and positive future.
- Live well. Remember that you have the power to put yourself in the place of feeling relief. You may not ever forget the experience, but you can put it in a place that does you no harm.
- Speak with a friend, therapist or clergy person if you still are having a difficult time. Sometimes writing the story down can help you clarify it and put the events and feelings in their proper perspective.

Forgiveness is the key to happiness.

The Course in Miracles

Sometimes when I am feeling pain, I don't realize that the cause of my pain is lack of forgiveness. Holding someone or something else accountable for my pain sometimes provides great instant temporary relief. However, when the pain doesn't go away, I know it is time to get to work and begin the process of forgiveness. My ego may hate it and would prefer that I enjoyed blaming. The more often and sooner that I reach for my forgiveness tools, however, the easier they become to use, and thus happiness comes more quickly. I have almost become addicted to quick relief. Hope you experience the same!

Activities: Is there a person or situation that has hurt you and you find hard to forgive? How does that make you feel? Take a deep breath. Write to this person or situation. Speak truthfully about your feelings. You probably don't want to send the letter. Read again the "Elements of Forgiveness" earlier in this chapter.

Affirmation: I know that forgiveness will give me freedom.

Giving And Receiving

"With our willingness to give that which we seek, we keep the abundance of the universe circulating in our lives."

—Deepak Chopra MD, Author, Teacher

Giving And Receiving

" Giving and receiving are one in truth."
Understanding this thought from the Course in Miracles has always been a work in progress in my life. When I was a child, our family always had plenty of money, and I gave it very little attention. I received what I wanted without having to give anything except a thank you and a smile.

When it was time for me to be responsible for my own finances, however, giving and receiving had different meanings. I had little confidence that I could control what money came in and what went out. Giving meant losing or becoming poorer and receiving meant getting or becoming richer. It seemed pretty simple but it was a very limiting belief. I realized later that it generated a lot of fear. What if no one was giving to me and I didn't have enough money to give to anyone else?

As time went on and I began to study higher spiritual thought, I knew there were other ways of looking at this dynamic. However, I still felt uneasy around money. I wanted it but felt powerless while handling it. It didn't make much difference as to my income. I never felt that I had enough.

As with many other women, I had developed the "bag lady syndrome." In fact, in a recent survey, it was found that one-half of women in America were afraid of becoming bag ladies, including women who were earning more than $100,000 a year. They were fearful they would have to eat cat food as they aged. For those of you who haven't experienced this, it is the fear that financial security can disappear in a heartbeat. It's the fear of not having any control. Because money comes magically, it can leave magically. Olivia Mellon, a therapist who specializes in money psychology, reports that men don't usually have these same fears.

Now I am older with more life experiences and thus more knowledge. I try to keep the bag lady in my past. When she does emerge, however, I tell her that I now a have new story to tell.

This story is about having the power to control the abundance in my life. I have this power because I am one with the all-creating force that creates my good. I realize that giving and receiving are inextricably linked together in the natural flow of life—like inhaling and exhaling. If I can inhale easily, I can exhale with ease. If I give with ease, I receive with ease.

Ten years ago, when I was receiving treatment for cancer, I was not able to work. Once I woke up in the middle of the night, very frightened that I would not have enough money to survive. Would I lose my house, car, have to beg for food? (Essentially the bag lady fears.) And besides that, would I die? After asking for guidance, I felt an urge to get up early that morning and go to the church that I had been attending. The maintenance man was in the yard raking leaves. I gave him a generous check to give to the minister.

All of a sudden, I felt incredibly powerful realizing that I was supporting the community that was providing me with spiritual support, so essential at this time. I was embracing control that I intuitively knew linked me to the Divine. What a miracle! A conviction of universal oneness was at the heart of this action;

thus when giving, I would not lose but receive more fully. And indeed, I did. I survived being jobless and a few months later, I began a new job making a higher salary than ever.

More recently, after retiring I realized that my writing projects were costing me more than I expected. Was I supposed to be doing these writing projects? If so, was the Divine going to provide me with the income that I needed? Having faith that the Divine was partnering with me, I asked for help. Two opportunities to easily receive income came my way. Within several months, I was receiving exactly what I had asked for.

> *My life has lightened and bright-ened up. I am in good health and have enhanced faith that abundance will always be in my life.*

Sometimes I enjoy paying for the person's cof-fee in the car in back of me at the drive up window at Starbucks. I pay and then drive off quickly. I receive such joy doing that and often feel a bit elfish. The next day a friend might offer to buy me lunch—or not. I forget to keep track sometimes as the gifts and receipts come so quickly.

I am now living more creatively with trust that I am taken care of. My life has become a wonderful adventure that enhances the joy I experience as well as the joy I bring to others.

The universe operates through dynamic exchange..giving and receiving are different aspects of the flow of energy in the universe

—Deepak Chopra

Activities: Write down a statement of how you see the giving and receiving balance in your life. Is it different than it was 20 years ago? Is there any way you would like to change that?

Affirmation: I am a strong and powerful person and have the ability to transform the experience of abundance in my life.

Ready For Dessert?

Thanks for sharing your time with me. I hope you have kept your fork and that my stories have inspired you to see your future as an expansive journey filled with the potential of many savory experiences. I read once that a writer's first responsibility is to foster and promote magic. I hope I have fostered some magic in you. When blended with your unique life experiences and creative genius, wonderful stories are sure to unfold.

It is important to remember that if we wait to feel totally confident before creating new stories in the second half of life, we may be relegated to sitting around for a really long time. If we enjoy our process and trust that our ignorance will lead to amazing new discoveries, we will find pleasure as we create. This is an opportunity to recognize our strengths without apology and use those strengths to direct and give energy to everything we do.

"Many people die with their music still in them. Why is this so? Too often it is because they are always getting ready to live. Before they know it, time runs out."

—Oliver Wendell Holmes

I always enjoy hearing from fellow travelers and would love to hear from you. If you would like to email me or to receive my e-newsletter, you may visit my website: www.barbwarner.com.

Following is a Celtic blessing written by John O'Donohue, best-selling author of *Anam Cara: A book of Celtic wisdom.*

A Blessing

May the light of your soul mind you,
May all your worry and anxiousness about becoming old be transfigured,
May you be given wisdom for the eye of your soul,
To see this beautiful time of harvesting.
May you have the commitment to harvest your life,

To heal what has hurt you, to allow it to come
Closer to you and become one with you.
May you have great dignity,
May you have a sense of how free you are,
And above all may you be given the wonderful
gift
Of meeting the eternal light and beauty that is
within you.
May you be blessed, and may you find a won-
derful love
In your self for your self.